Ladakhi

5

INDIGENOUS PEOPLES OF THE WORLD
Ladakhi

Grolier Educational Corporation
SHERMAN TURNPIKE, DANBURY, CONNECTICUT 06816

Published by Grolier Educational Corporation 1995
Sherman Turnpike, Danbury, CT 06816

Set ISBN: 0-7172-7470-5
Volume ISBN: *Ladakhi* 0-7172-7481-0
Library of Congress Number 94-079535

Manufactured in the United States of America.

Contributors

Jennifer Croft *(Ladakhi)* holds a degree in anthropology from Columbia University and is an editor and free-lance writer.

Anne Johnson *(Inuit, Karenni, Mentawai, Naga)* holds a degree from the University of Wisconsin, Madison. She has done extensive research on myths and folk epics from around the world.

Barbara Miller *(Tuareg)* is a Ph.D. candidate in anthropology at New York University. She specializes in ethnographic filmmaking. She has conducted applied urban research and has been involved with developing curricula for museums and schools.

Eugene Murphy, Ph.D. *(Maya)* is an instructor of anthropology at Columbia University. He has produced an ethnographic documentary on Mayan migration and has written extensively on the peoples of Mexico and China.

Roger Rosen *(Endangered Peoples)* is an editor and publisher. He has published material on the indigenous peoples of the former Soviet Union and has edited numerous articles and papers on the plight of indigenous peoples.

Steven Rubenstein, Ph.D. *(Huaorani)* has been awarded grants in the field of anthropology from the Guggenheim, Fulbright, and MacArthur Foundations and has conducted fieldwork in Brazil, Ecuador, and the United States.

Colleen She *(Miao)* received a master's degree in East Asian studies from Columbia University. She is a free-lance writer and translator.

Jeanne Strazzabosco *(Wayana)* is an instructor in French and Spanish and a free-lance translator and writer whose work regularly addresses the plight of indigenous peoples.

Pegi Vail *(Omo Peoples)* is a Ph.D. candidate in anthropology at New York University. She specializes in visual anthropology and has worked extensively with children's educational programs at museums and schools.

Contents

The Ladakhi people take great pride in their culture. This young woman wears traditional clothes in celebration of the appointment of the new governor of Leh, the largest city in Ladakh.

CHAPTER 1

ON A MOUNTAIN TRAIL

DOLMA TUGS AT THE COLLAR OF HER WOOL SHIRT, WHICH IS starting to scratch as she climbs the steep mountain. It was so cold when she left the village this morning that she had to dress warmly, but now that she has been hiking for an hour and the sun is rising, she wishes she had worn something lighter, such as the bright red sweatshirt her uncle had brought her from the city of Leh. Dolma has never been to the city, but her uncle says that the street bazaar is lined with stalls selling Western-style clothing, electronic devices, ice cream.

Dolma stops to catch her breath at a place where the trail flattens out slightly. She finds a smooth rock to sit on and looks out at the land below. Although she has seen this view hundreds of times in her young life, it never fails to take her breath away. It is especially beautiful now, in the early morning sunlight that bathes the valley floor in a soft glow. Below, Dolma can see a cluster of white, two-story houses surrounded by trees; this is her village. Her family's house is the one with the large apricot tree next to it. Beyond the village, the valley floor stretches for miles, rising slowly to the hills. Beyond the hills, though she can barely see them, lie snow-capped mountain peaks that seem to touch the clouds.

The villagers' animals graze in the valley, on the grazing land called the *phu*. Dolma's brother, Dalip, is almost old enough to be responsible for leading the animals to pasture. But Dolma knows that Dalip has other ideas. He would rather go with their uncle to the city and get a paying job in a hotel or restaurant. He has suggested that Dolma come too; she could easily get a job as a tour guide or a waitress, because she is friendly and learns other languages quickly. But Dolma isn't sure she wants to leave the village where her family has lived for so many generations.

The sound of voices coming down the trail brings Dolma back to reality. She looks up and sees one of the Buddhist priests, or lamas, coming toward her. Dolma and the lama bow slightly to greet each other. "You are working today?" he asks.

"Yes," says Dolma. "Do you think there will be many visitors?"

"Yes, I think so," the lama says. "I hope it is a successful day for you."

"Thank you," says Dolma. She hoists her bag to her shoulder and walks on. The more visitors come to the monastery, the more money she will make with the postcards she sells there. It was her uncle's idea: He brings the postcards from the city, and Dolma sells them to the foreign tourists who come in bus-loads to the monastery every day. When her parents were growing up, a young woman would never have thought of

Like many Ladakhi youth, this boy is responsible for the care of his family's herds. He leads the animals to lower, warmer pastures for the winter.

leaving her village every day to go to work; it was assumed that she would help her family at home and in the fields. But for Dolma, making money seems a necessity. She and her family want many things that cost money. And many girls in the village are not as lucky as Dolma. They cannot find jobs. That is why many leave for the city, as Dalip wants to do.

The sun now feels hot on Dolma's neck as she nears the monastery. She is already tired from the long walk, and she will be on her feet all day. She looks forward to going down the trail again, many hours later, under the setting sun. ▲

CHAPTER 2

A REMOTE AND RUGGED LAND

LADAKH IS A REGION IN THE FAR NORTH OF INDIA, ABOVE THE Himalaya mountain range. It is a high-altitude desert, with wide valleys punctuated by hills and mountains and dotted with pristine turquoise lakes. The major mountain ranges in Ladakh are the Zanskar, Karakoram, and Ladakh ranges, where peaks rise as high as 20,000 feet. The jagged peaks of the Himalayas block rainclouds traveling north, and this keeps the region dry.

Ladakh spans an area of about 40,000 square miles and has a population of about 150,000, most of whom are Ladakhi. The largest city in the region is Leh. Bordering Ladakh is the Chang Tang, a vast, high plateau on the border between Tibet and India. The Chang Tang is known for its harsh winds that can bury travelers in drifts of snow. Because of Chinese repression, nomadic pastoral peoples who inhabited the Chang Tang have fled Tibet and now share the Ladakhis' fields.

The climate of Ladakh does not seem to have been created with people in mind. Winter lasts seven months, and summer

Nestled in the Himalayan mountain range in northern India lies the city of Leh.

is short; temperatures fluctuate wildly, even in the course of a day, which is typically windy and sunny. Ladakh is in one of the sunniest areas in the world. Rainfall is rare, generally no more than three inches a year. The main source of water for most of the region's people is snowmelt. The sunlight is incredibly intense and provides scorching heat in summer, when daytime temperatures may climb as high as 100°F. On summer nights, however, the temperature may fall to a chilly 32°F. Winter has similar variations, with daytime highs of 35°-40°F and lows of -30°F or -40°F. During winter, the entire

Although Ladakh may appear to be barren, it harbors a wealth of flora and wildlife from which the Ladakhi people draw their bounty.

area is frozen solid, and fierce winds can erupt into tornadoes. In a remarkable instance of human adaptation, the Ladakhi people have developed a comfortable existence over the centuries despite the region's extreme climatic conditions.

Vegetation and Wildlife

Ladakh may look bleak and desolate at first glance, but this apparent bleakness conceals a rich and bountiful natural world. Ladakh's harsh climate supports a surprising number of sturdy plant and animal species. At low elevations, willow and poplar trees are common. Wild plants and herbs such as edelweiss, blue poppy, rose, and cappari abound in summer. Some of these plants are used for practical purposes. For example, a species of honeysuckle provides the thick rope used by the Ladakhi to make hanging bridges. Many wild herbs are used for their medicinal properties.

At Ladakh's highest altitudes live blue sheep, wolves, and snow leopards, which are extremely rare. Few people have seen more than the footprints of the cunning snow leopard, which is the most endangered of all the large cats. It is also the most formidable predator of the region, making it an enemy of Ladakhi shepherds. Only the adult yak is too large for it to tackle. The snow leopard's body is built for climbing the rocky terrain, and its coat provides perfect camouflage. Before the snow leopard population was decimated by fur poachers, it roamed a territory spanning over half a million square miles. Poaching is now illegal, but a dozen snow leopard skins are still smuggled from Ladakh each year, and the animals' bones are sold in China for use in aphrodisiacs.

Other animals found in the region include wild goat, red bear, wild horse, white lynx, Tibetan antelope, gazelle, marmot, ibex, and hare. The streams support large numbers of fish, and birds such as the ibisbill, rosefinch, snowfinch, huge bearded vulture, and rock pigeon are abundant. Every spring, bar-headed geese migrate to Tso Morari, a lake in one of Ladakh's most remote areas. These birds have the largest wingspan of any geese, which enables them to fly over some of the world's highest peaks.

Life at High Altitude

Both animals and humans have had to adapt over thousands of years to Ladakh's forbidding conditions. High altitude is one of the conditions that make life in Ladakh challenging. The air in most regions contains only half the amount of oxygen found in air at sea level. Visitors to Ladakh find it difficult to breathe and are often ill for the first part of their visits, a condition known as high-altitude hypoxia. Yet the Ladakhi are able to perform all manner of daily activities and even carry out strenuous work in the thin air. Scientists have found that their bodies have adapted to the conditions. Their blood contains greater amounts of hemoglobin, so it can actually capture and carry more oxygen than that of people living at lower altitudes. ▲

CHAPTER 3

A CONTESTED REGION

LADAKH WAS AN INDEPENDENT KINGDOM FOR MANY HUNDREDS of years. Its name probably comes from the Tibetan phrase *la dags*, which means "land of mountain passes." The kingdom was founded by Tatar herders about 2,000 years ago. It is believed that the Tatars have the same origins as Native Americans; both have been traced to the area near Lake Baikal in present-day Siberia and the Gobi Desert in Central Asia. A few cultural and linguistic traits also point to common origins. For example, the staple of the Ladakhi diet is a barley flour the Ladakhi call *ngamphe*; the word for it in Tibetan is *tsampa*, and *samp* is the word used by the Algonkian peoples of North America for a similar food made of corn.

The first people to live in Ladakh were probably the Mon, from northern India, and the Dard, from Gilgit in present-day Pakistan. The Dard claim to be descendants of the Macedonian conqueror Alexander the Great (356-323 BC), who led his men into northern India. In about 5000 BC Mongolian nomads may have come to the region via Tibet.

Modern-day Ladakhi are probably an ethnic mix of these three groups. Tibetan (Mahayana) Buddhism came to Ladakh about 2,000 years ago and is the dominant religion today. The Chinese pilgrim Fa-Hien found Buddhism flourishing in Ladakh when he visited in about 400 AD.

At various times throughout history, rulers of the neighboring Muslim state of Kashmir have considered Ladakh to be within their authority. In the 15th and 16th centuries Ladakh was invaded several times by the Kashmiri. It was invaded by Tibetans in 1646, and the king of Ladakh turned to the Mughal emperor of India for help. The Tibetans were defeated by the Mughals in 1650. Deldan Nangyal, the ruler of Ladakh at the time, accepted Islam, and a mosque was built in Leh in 1665. Ladakh fell under the rule of the Sikhs when they conquered Kashmir in 1819. In 1834, Ladakh was invaded by the Hindu Dogra of India, who gained control of Kashmir and placed Ladakh under the jurisdiction of the new Indian state known as Jammu and Kashmir. Great Britain gained control over much of India starting in the 17th century, increasing its hold over time. In 1947, the British-administered partition of India and Pakistan also resulted in Ladakh being granted its current status as a semiautonomous district. Pakistan and India each govern a portion of Ladakh. Ladakh is divided into a mainly Buddhist region (Leh) and a predominantly Muslim region (Kargil).

Because of its location, Ladakh has always been a major focus of Central Asian trade and has had political, religious, and

Most Ladakhi are Buddhists. Here young women participate in an annual Buddhist celebration in honor of the Dalai Lama.

commercial connections with neighboring states. An important feeder route on China's Silk Road ran through Ladakh, and for centuries it attracted Mongol, Chinese, Kashmiri, Kyrgyz, and Afghan traders, who brought caravans of goods to be sold or exchanged in Leh. However, this was stopped by the Chinese government when troops sealed the common border with Ladakh in 1949. Ladakh's relations with Tibet were completely severed in 1962 because of further Chinese aggression.

Ladakh is now regarded as strategically important by the Indian government because of increasing tension with Pakistan and China. The Chinese have attempted several times to alter Ladakh's borders. Chinese troops clashed with Indian border patrols in 1958; in 1959, an Indian patrol was attacked by the Chinese army, and nine Indians were killed. In 1962, the Chinese seized an area of Ladakh's sparsely populated north-east corner called Aksai Chin, and as a result Ladakh lost 40 percent of its original size. This prompted the Indian government to take a greater military interest in the area. They began to construct a road between Leh and Srinagar, the capital of Kashmir. The Indian military presence in Ladakh increased.▲

CHAPTER 4

THE PEOPLE OF "LITTLE TIBET"

WHILE LADAKH IS MADE UP OF ABOUT A DOZEN RELIGIOUS and ethnic groups—including Sikhs, Muslims, Hindus, Christians, and Tibetans—the unifying cultural influence is Tibetan. In fact, Ladakh is sometimes referred to as "Little Tibet." Ladakhi language, art, architecture, medicine, and music all have Tibetan roots. Ethnic Ladakhi (also known as Bhot, Bod, Bodh, Bot-pa, Bota, and Bhautta), speak a language called Bodhi. Although it is related to Tibetan, it is different enough to be a separate language.

In an environment that may strike outsiders as bleak and lifeless, the Ladakhi have managed for centuries to sustain a comfortable lifestyle. Part of their secret seems to be the frugality in their traditional way of life. Virtually everything used by the Ladakhi comes from the earth and is returned to the earth in some way. They live as self-sufficient farmers, getting everything they need from their crops and domestic animals. Even human waste is used as garden fertilizer after being mixed with ash and dirt. Homespun robes are worn until they are

The Ladakhi allow nothing to go to waste. They have learned to use and replace all that they take from the earth.

utterly worn out, and even then they are put to another use: When packed with mud, they prevent leaks in irrigation channels. The Ladakhi are dependent on the outside world only for salt, tea, and a few metals.

Agriculture

The Ladakhi depend on the products of their crops and the work of their domestic animals. Only a few crops grow in the cold mountain air. The main crops grown in Ladakh are barley, peas, turnips, and potatoes. At lower elevations it is possible to grow black walnut, apple, and apricot trees. The soil is thin; water must be cleverly channeled to the fields through intricate canals that capture the snowmelt. That enough food can be grown to sustain life is an amazing accomplishment.

The planting of crops is a festive occasion for the community because it signifies the end of winter. Communal labor—everyone pitching in—gets the job done. Depending on the altitude, this work begins sometime between February and June. A *nyitho*, an obelisk-shaped pile of stones, serves as the agricultural calendar. When the sun is judged to be in the proper place, an *onpo* or astrologer studies his charts to determine an auspicious day for sowing. A feast is prepared to pacify *sadak* and *lhu*, the earth and water spirits. Milk and other offerings are thrown into the stream for the spirits' benefit. Buddhist monks recite prayers for an entire day.

Weeks before the day designated for sowing, donkeys bring loads of manure to the side of the field. At dawn on the day of sowing, women spread the manure. They are joined by the rest of the family later in the morning: The men carry the wooden ploughs, and the children lead the dzo (a hybrid of Asian cow and yak). The work is hard, but the air is festive; the people sing and laugh and drink *chang*, a home-brewed barley beer.

Once the crop has been planted, it needs only to be watered. In most villages, an appointed or elected official called a *churpon* operates the flow of water.

Harvest

Harvest, like the sowing of crops, is an occasion for celebration.

In the evening during harvest time, people gather to sing, drink, and dance. Every activity of the harvest has its own song. Garlands of wheat, barley, and peas decorate houses.

First, villagers of all ages cut the crop with sickles. It is then piled in sheaves and carried to the threshing floor in loads on people's backs. The threshing floor is a large circle of packed earth, about thirty feet in diameter. Animals, usually dzo, are attached by rope to a pole in the middle of the threshing floor. While a thresher shouts or sings words of encouragement, the animals walk in a circle to trample the crop, threshing the grain. Bending down to munch on the crop is permitted behavior!

Winnowing is the next step in the process. The crop is thrown up into the air with wooden forks by two people facing each other. The chaff blows away in the wind, while the grain falls to the ground. After this step, the grain is sifted and stored in sacks. Some crops, such as peas, are stored on the roofs of houses; the air in Ladakh is so cold and dry that the roof can serve as an outdoor refrigerator.

After the harvest, food is stored for the long winter. Because the growing season is so short, the Ladakhi perform heavy agricultural work for only a few months. They spend the rest of the year caring for their animals, cooking, carrying water, spinning wool, and enjoying many festivals and celebrations. Because the Ladakhi rely on simple tools, animals, and teamwork rather than high-technology tools, each project takes a relatively long time to complete. But the Ladakhi do not seem

The agricultural year is short, and much time is spent tending animals.

While a diet rich in butter and salt may be considered by the Western world to be un-healthful, the Ladakhi have made these foods staples and are strong and healthy for it.

to mind; they work at their own pace and enjoy their leisure time when they have it. They are particularly fond of archery and hold archery competitions at which the winners receive cash prizes. These competitions are celebrated with dancing, singing, and the drinking of *chang*.

The Traditional Diet

The Ladakhi eat few fruits or green vegetables, because such things do not grow well in their climate. They consume a great deal of butter and salt.

The staple of the Ladakhi diet is *ngamphe*, a roasted barley flour which, when water is added, becomes a ready-to-eat food. Barley flour has many uses for the Ladakhi; unroasted, it is mixed into soup or added to dried pea flour, and any extra is made into *chang*. Wheat is used to make bread, which is cooked on the stove or roasted over ashes. Yak milk, which is very rich, is usually made into butter and cheese. The cheese, called *churpe*, is dried and hardened in the sun and can be stored for the whole winter. Meat can also be dried and stored.

The Ladakhi consume large amounts of green tea, which is brewed with butter and salt. The brew seems to be another example of Ladakhi adaptation to their environment. The butter serves to moisten the lips, which can become chapped after a day in the sun and wind, and the salt replenishes what is lost after a hard day of physical work.

Animals

The domesticated animals of the Ladakhi are critical to their ability to live above subsistence level. These animals provide them with meat, wool, milk, butter and cheese, labor, and transport. They also provide fuel in the form of dried dung cakes, which are used for cooking fuel and heat. Predictably, their domestic animals are hardy breeds that can withstand the cold temperatures, high altitudes, and rocky landscape. Sheep, goats, donkeys, shaggy horses, and dzo are the most common animals. Fish, while plentiful in local streams, are never eaten. The Ladakhi believe that it is better to take as few lives as possible. Many fish would have to die to feed as many people as a single large slaughtered animal. Being Buddhists, the Ladakhis regard very seriously the taking of an animal's life and ask for forgiveness and say prayers before any animal is killed.

The shepherding of animals, like the harvesting of crops, is done communally. A shepherd, usually a young male from the village, leads the animals to the grazing land, the *phu*. A *phu* that is far from the village may have a small stone house where the shepherd can spend the night. In many villages, the animals are taken to warmer, lower valleys during the winter.

The coarse hair and wool of the goat and yak are spun for blankets, shoes, sacks, and rope. Men generally make these items, whereas women spin the finer wool of sheep, which is made into clothing. Spinning wool seems to be an almost meditative activity for many Ladakhi, who spin whenever time allows, sometimes even while walking! The finest wool produced by the Ladakhi is sometimes exported to the neighboring Indian state of Jammu and Kashmir.

Division of Labor

The efficient domestic economy of the Ladakhi is based on cooperation among members of the community, who work together to get things done. Everyone knows his or her tasks. For example, young people are responsible for ploughing, sowing, carrying compost, harvesting, cutting grass, preparing bricks, constructing fences and walls, bringing water, digging

Young people are responsible for many tasks, including shepherding the animals.

water channels, winnowing, and threshing. Ploughing is the only activity performed exclusively by men; all other tasks are shared by men and women equally. In addition to these tasks, women are also responsible for cooking and preparing tea and *chang*. Even the elderly have work to do: They may baby-sit, weave, tend the grazing cattle, rotate the house prayer wheel, and make shoes, socks, ropes, or other items.

The position of women in traditional Ladakhi society seems to be quite strong. In the traditional Ladakhi economy, most activity takes place in the informal sector. In this system,

Everyone takes part in the work to be done such as weaving the cloth that people wear.

women's domestic work and work in the fields is as critical to the functioning of the economy as is the ploughing performed by men. That is changing, however, as more men take wage jobs and begin to participate in a market economy. The important tasks involved in managing a household are considered less important, because they do not bring in money in the formal sense. Women's status is suffering as a result, as they are seen as less productive members of society.

The Oneness of Life
Like Tibetans, the people of Ladakh overwhelmingly practice Tibetan Mahayana Buddhism and consider the Dalai Lama

to be their spiritual leader. One of the principal beliefs of Buddhism is that everything in the world is impermanent, so human beings must remain unattached to the trappings of earthly existence.

Another tenet of Buddhism is that reality is circular: Life and death, for example, are simply two parts of a constant process, not a beginning or an ending. Everything is connected to everything else: A flower is not simply a flower, but a product of the soil, rain, wind, and weather. It is made up of a series of relationships rather than being a defined object in itself. Happiness can best be achieved by understanding that everything exists because of processes beyond our control. The belief that we even have an independent self is seen as a barrier to achieving happiness, because the self is never satisfied, just as we can never really be satisfied by material things. Compassion, then, is a way to recognize that all human beings and, indeed, all living things are connected to each other.

The Ladakhi devotion to Buddhism is evident everywhere. At the entrance to every village is a twenty-foot spire of whitewashed stone and mud called a _chorten_. A common symbol of Tibetan Buddhism, the _chorten_ contains relics of Buddha or especially revered lamas. On top of the spire is a crescent moon cradling the sun: This represents the unity of two things we normally think of as being totally separate and thus symbolizes the oneness of all life. Prayer flags flutter over houses. They are never taken down; they are left to spread their message in the winds. The Ladakhi practice Buddhism on an everyday

Most Ladakhi villages have a Buddhist monastery nearby, like this one near the village of Lamayuru.

basis, by making prayers and offerings in their homes, and with weekly, monthly, and yearly celebrations of occasions such as the birthday of Guru Rinpoche, who brought Buddhism to Tibet from India.

A Buddhist monastery, or *gonpa*, is perched on a hill in almost every Ladakhi village. The monastery serves an important social and economic function. Some monasteries own land that is harvested by the villagers; sometimes a portion of the village harvest is donated to the monastery. In this way, the people of the village provide the monks with food in exchange for the monks' religious services to the community. In turn, the monastery takes care of children who cannot be supported by their families. In the monastery the children receive room, board, education, and an occupation. In fact, anyone, regardless of age or sex, can opt for the life of a monk or nun and practice celibacy and religious devotion for life. In the monastery, the monks spend their time studying, chanting scriptures, and learning languages before taking their vows. They also learn to play musical instruments and sing songs against evil spirits.▲

CHAPTER 5

FAMILY AND COMMUNITY

THE BUDDHIST PRINCIPLES OF COOPERATION AND COM-
passion are reflected in everyday Ladakhi interactions. Village
strife is rare, and if it occurs, a third party generally steps in
to mediate the dispute. Many Ladakhi embrace the belief that
because they must live together, they should try to live as har-
moniously as possible. Families must practice this cooperation
as well, as several generations often live under one roof.

Village Life

Traditional villages are run in a democratic manner. A *goba*,
or village head, is appointed by the village. In larger villages,
the *goba* presides over a village council, a group of appointed
representatives from different *chutsos* (groups of ten houses).
The size of a village varies according to the availability of water
at a given site.

Families generally own their own land, about five acres per
family. However, the Ladakhi concept of land-owning is different
from the Western notion of private property. The "owner" of

Ladakhi houses are made from stone and mud bricks.

the land is more like a guardian, because it is believed that no one has an absolute claim to the land. Land is kept in one piece as it is passed down through the generations, as opposed to being split up among heirs. Ladakhi families are generally small, and the eldest son is usually the recipient of the family land.

When a Ladakhi family builds a house, a high lama, who has been granted special distinction by the Dalai Lama, comes to bless the land. The first floor of a house is often made of stone. The floor area may be quite large, spanning as much as

4,000 square feet. The rest of the house is constructed of mud bricks, which the whole family make together. Even small children pitch in, pressing the mud into wooden molds. The bricks are ready for use after a few weeks of drying in the sun. To keep out the bitter cold, the walls may be as much as three feet thick. Two or three stories are built and topped with a flat roof of poplar beams layered with willow branches. A shrub called *yagdzas*, similar to heather, is placed on top of the wood. The final step is to pack the layers with mud and dirt. This type of roof is said to last a hundred years. Because there is so little precipitation, any snow is simply brushed off. The Ladakhi and Native Americans share the tradition of constructing their dwellings to face east, toward the sunrise. Ladakhi houses are quite beautiful with their whitewashed walls, carved balconies, and carved lintels over some windows and doors.

The large size of Ladakhi houses can be attributed to the need for space to store food for the long winter. The ground floor is usually made up of stables for the animals. The kitchen, the largest room in most houses, is where the family spends most of their time. A large, shiny black stove provides warmth. Each house also has a small chapel with a carved altar, silver bowls, family treasures, and books. This room is used for praying and making offerings.

Instead of surnames, Ladakhi are identified by house names or titles. A house name is usually derived from the ecological setting in which the house is located. For example, a house near a stream may be called Tokpopa because *tok* means "stream" and *popa* means "those near it." Because the house names signify land ownership, they are useful for village accounting purposes.

Marriage and Family

A unique feature of traditional Ladakhi society is the practice of polyandry as the preferred form of marriage. Polyandry means that a woman is married to several men at a time, sometimes to men who are brothers. Polyandry was declared illegal in 1942 by the Indian government; although the practice continues, it has steadily declined, with monogamy becoming more common. Polygyny, in which a man has more than one wife, is also practiced to some extent. It often occurs when a woman is not able to bear children. A second wife, usually her sister, marries into the family to provide offspring.

Anthropologists suspect that polyandry is society's way of controlling population in an environment where the earth can sustain only a limited number of people. Hill peoples who live under similar conditions in Nepal and Tibet also maintain small, stable populations. With more husbands for each wife, some Ladakhi women do not have husbands and are thus removed from the reproducing population. Often these women become Buddhist nuns, many of whom live at home and enjoy a high degree of flexibility. They are indistinguishable from other family members except that they wear their hair short and spend more time in prayer. The high number of Buddhist monks in Ladakh also removes a certain number of males from the marriage pool. A family may choose the marriage option that is best

Ladakhi children live with their parents in small families. The Ladakhi tend to keep their families small because the land cannot support many people.

for them depending on how many people can be supported by their land.

As winter is a time when the Ladakhi are able to relax and celebrate, weddings occur most frequently during this season. When a young person approaches marriageable age, a potential spouse is sought out by parents, relatives, and family friends. Initially, a boy's family sends gifts to the house of his chosen bride. If these gifts are accepted, the relatives of the engaged couple arrange the details of the wedding. The date of the wedding is decided by the *onpo*, or astrologer. On the wedding day, according to custom, a group of relatives or friends of the groom come to the house of the bride and stand shouting outside her door, "forcing" her to come out. She emerges, crying on cue, and the wedding proceeds.

The Phasphun

The strong commitment to cooperation among the Ladakhi people has given rise to a unique institution called the *phasphun*. The *phasphun* is a group of families who vow to provide assistance to each other during important life-cycle events such as birth, marriage, and death. When a person dies, for example, family members are not allowed to touch the body; the *phasphun*, instead, take care of all arrangements. Only they are allowed to touch the deceased. They remove the clothing, bathe the body, and arrange it in a sitting position, with hands folded. (The sitting position is believed by the Ladakhi to save fuel during the cremation.) Then the body is dressed in white and placed in a sack. According to tradition, it is then placed in a corner of the house for a period of time determined by the lamas. Generally, the higher the social standing of the family, the longer the body stays in the house. If the weather is cold enough, this period can be as long as a month. The *phasphun* also act as hosts during the funeral and carry the body to the cremation site. The husband or wife of the deceased is not allowed to cross any water channels for a month following the death, so during this time he or she might go to stay at the home of a *phasphun* family.

The *phasphun* also provide assistance during the birth of a baby. In fact, birth usually takes place at the home of a *phasphun*, but only if going to such a home does not require the pregnant woman and her husband to cross any channels of water. If an appropriate *phasphun* residence cannot be found, a tent is set up so that the child is not born in the house. The *phasphun* and relatives attend a celebration called Nang-Dan, which is held after the birth.

Somewhat similar to the *phasphun* relationship is the *chhasphun*, in which two people from different families agree to help each other in time of need. They are considered as siblings.

Medicine and Healing

As with many indigenous peoples, the shaman plays a very important role in Ladakhi society. A shaman is someone who can communicate with the spirit world. Spirits, known as *lhas*, are believed to have healing powers. Among the Ladakhi, a shaman can be either a man or a woman and is known as a *lhaba*, meaning wiseman or wisewoman.

In 1981, a German doctor named Walter A. Frank was cured by a female shaman in the town of Sabu in northern Ladakh. Dr. Frank was suffering from viral bronchitis and sinusitis. The *lhaba*, dressed in a ceremonial costume, seemed to go into a trance. She placed a tube against his chest. Then she appeared to suck out a black fluid. Dr. Frank reported that after this treatment his respiratory tract was free and clear, and he felt as if he had never been sick.

The trancelike state of the *lhaba* during a healing is believed to be caused by the spirits speaking through him or her. The *lhaba* may begin a loud, unearthly chant, sometimes even shouting at patients.

A practitioner of Tibetan medicine known as an *amchi* lives in every Ladakhi village. The *amchi* diagnoses illnesses by taking a patient's pulse in six places on each side of the body. Healing minerals and plants are administered in the form of powders, tablets, and special foods. Surgery is rarely practiced, because it is rumored that centuries ago a queen of Ladakh was accidentally killed during surgery. Stitches are not generally used either. In traditional Ladakhi society, however, accidents are rare because there are few cars or hazardous machines.

The village *onpo* may also treat illnesses using a book of astrological computations. His remedies usually include reading sacred books or performing a prayer service.▲

CHAPTER 6

CONTACT WITH FOREIGNERS

BECAUSE OF LADAKH'S LOCATION ON THE SILK ROAD, THE Ladakhi, especially in Leh, were accustomed to visitors who came to the area to trade. Generally these visitors were from neighboring countries, sometimes from as far away as Russia. The difficulty of entering Ladakh over the Himalayas kept it relatively isolated from the south.

The first Englishman to enter Leh was a British veterinarian, William Moorcroft, in 1820. Moorcroft was doing research for the East India Company, sponsored by the British government. Moorcroft's research was twofold: He wanted to find suitable horses for the East India Company's cavalry, and he wanted to explore the possibilities of trading with India's neighbors and gaining an advantage over Russia in the process.

Missionary Activity

In 1855, missionaries from Germany's Moravian Church came to Ladakh. The missionaries interacted with the Ladakhi for 30 years before founding a mission in Leh in 1885. Six years

German missionaries attempted to impose Christianity on the Ladakhi traditional religion. They had very little luck converting Ladakhi from Buddhism.

later, the two resident missionaries died of typhus. Another mission was established in 1899 in Kalatse (Khalsi), a three-day journey from Leh. Some of the more positive activities of the mission included translating religious texts from Bodhi into Tibetan, providing medical care, and writing histories of the area. The governor of Kashmir, Radha Kishan, issued an edict requiring that every family with more than one child send a student to the mission school. Among the courses offered by the mission school were Tibetan, Urdu, English, geography, nature study, arithmetic, and half an hour of voluntary Bible study. An incentive for attending the mission school became clear: Its students were more likely to obtain prestigious jobs in the Kashmiri government. The influence of the mission schools decreased over time, as government schools were opened in 1911.

The missionaries had little luck in converting the Buddhist Ladakhi. To some extent, the Ladakhi believed, all religions were the same; why, then, should they abandon one in favor of the other? Also, religion was seen as the professional concern of the monkhood, so the missionaries' Christian message fell on deaf ears. The few people who did convert often had to defy their families to do so. Ladakh as a whole never even came close to becoming Christian; Buddhism was too ingrained in their culture and their everyday beliefs.

The Growth of Tourism

Aside from the missionaries, Ladakh was relatively isolated from outside contact until 1974. Until that time, the area was restricted by the Indian government and was closed to foreigners. Once the area was opened, however, tourists began arriving in increasing numbers. In 1979, regular flights began in and out of Ladakh, and 1984 saw the arrival of 15,000 tourists.

It is ironic that Ladakh's reputation as an idyllic enclave of Tibetan Buddhism made the region attractive to tourists, because tourism itself has been responsible for making Ladakh increasingly less idyllic. The growth of tourism necessitated the building of hotels, restaurants, and shops. Ladakh had to rely on outside help to supply labor and products for the

The German missionaries were not successful in their efforts to convert the Ladakhi to Christianity. With Buddhism such an integral part of their culture and society, the Ladakhi saw no reason to adopt a new religion. These novice monks are deciphering sacred texts in one of the many monasteries in Ladakh.

tourist industry. Kashmiri, Nepali, and Tibetan refugees staff many hotels. Airlines, transport companies, tour operators, travel agencies, and souvenir importers are often Indian-owned. Thus, the Ladakhi themselves have not seen a profit commensurate with the growth of tourism. In fact, they have had to deal with steady inflation and a situation in which their traditional institutions are treated as curiosities. Religious sites such as monasteries are marked with signs, and entrepreneurs sell tickets for admission. Tourists are sometimes given priority at religious feasts because they are willing to pay a fee. Some religious festivals traditionally held in winter are celebrated in summer to capitalize on the tourist season. Some lamas have lost the respect of the people because they have become agents of free enterprise, charging tourists for the privilege of seeing certain objects or places.

Tourism has also intensified tensions between Ladakh's Buddhists and the Kashmiri Muslims who have come to Ladakh to take advantage of the tourist trade. The number of Muslims in Leh has increased, and the ratio of Muslims to Buddhists is nearly one to one. Buddhist Ladakhi have accused the Muslims of stretching resources that are already pinched and creating a competitive situation between Buddhists and Muslims. Many Ladakhi have had to take jobs with outsiders to make a living. At some monasteries frequented by tourists, monks have complained of Muslims posing as tour guides. These so-called guides, the monks charge, have encouraged tourists to steal relics and *tankhas*, painted scrolls, and have provided them with misinformation about the religious sites.

Muslim-Buddhist Tension

The tension exacerbated by the tourist industry came to a head in 1989, when violence broke out between Buddhists and Muslims at a bazaar in Leh. Indian police opened fire in an attempt to control the situation, killing three Buddhist demonstrators and a Muslim villager. Much of Ladakh was placed under curfew by the police. In 1991, violent riots erupted in Leh;

shops, hotels, and other tourist establishments were stoned and forced to shut down. Both Muslim and Buddhist grievances contributed to the violence. Many Buddhists believed that the Muslim-dominated government of Kashmir was discriminating against them and favoring the local Muslims. Many Muslims, on the other hand, perceived that they had to defend their interests against the Buddhist majority.

In a move that can only contribute to the divisive atmosphere, the Ladakh Buddhist Association has declared a social and economic boycott of Muslims, in some cases even splitting up families with marital links to Muslims. Even tourists have felt the impact of Muslim-Buddhist conflict: Some have been warned to ride only in taxis driven by Buddhists, or else they will not be allowed into the monasteries.

The Ladakhi, who number about 150,000, have as neighbors about eight million predominantly Muslim Kashmiri, who lead the state government in the city of Srinagar. The Kashmiri are themselves currently waging a violent movement to secede from India and establish Kashmir as an independent Muslim state. The Ladakhi have had to deal with their proximity to a volatile situation and to the economic toll it has taken on the Kashmiri government. The fighting that broke out in 1990 between Kashmiri separatists and Indian army soldiers in Kashmir has caused even more tourists to visit Ladakh.

Pakistan and India have agreed to begin a dialogue on the issue of Kashmiri independence. For predominantly Buddhist Ladakh, of course, the ideal situation would be to remain part of the secular Indian state rather than becoming part of a Muslim nation. The Ladakhi must work with the Indian government in New Delhi to insure that Ladakh will be able to protect its interests in the face of Kashmiri nationalism.▲

CHAPTER 7

DEVELOPMENT AND CHANGE

TOURISM HAS NOT BEEN THE ONLY FACTOR TAKING A TOLL ON traditional Ladakhi institutions. Economic development policies advanced by the Indian government, well-meaning as they might be, have not always been positive developments for Ladakh. In some cases, this is because such policies are not developed by those who know Ladakh best. They are decided by either the state government of Kashmir or the central government in Delhi, not by Ladakhi officials. Also, the policies are carried out by non-Ladakhi who in many cases do not even speak the local language. The Indian development commissioner assigned to Ladakh, for example, spends only a few years at his or her job—hardly enough time to get to learn Ladakhi culture in any depth.

The model of development that has been imposed on the Ladakhi assumes a Western notion of progress. Western-style education and medicine, for example, have been introduced without an attempt to incorporate them into traditional knowledge. Ladakhi children are taught in English or Urdu at the

There is some concern that foreign values are being imposed on Ladakhi children attending government-run schools.

expense of their native tongue. Hundreds of young Muslim teachers have been brought in from Kashmir to teach at Ladakhi schools, bringing to bear a new cultural influence and, many believe, imposing their own value system in the process. While literacy in itself is certainly a positive development, the question is whether it is being introduced in a way that bolsters or degrades traditional institutions. In an attempt to counteract outside influences, the Students' Educational and Cultural Movement of Ladakh sponsors regular cultural shows in an attempt to sustain Ladakhi traditions for young people.

Growth caused by the tourist industry and increased exposure to the outside world have made Ladakh today look very different from the Ladakh that remained relatively unchanged for hundreds of years. Leh has grown rapidly; the population has doubled in the last 16 years. The city now boasts a gas station, a hospital, banks, movie theaters, even a football stadium. A growing police force has been accompanied by an expanding court system.

The detrimental effects of such modernization are more subtle. The growth of a formal economic sector has pushed increasing numbers of Ladakhi into the market economy. Rather than growing subsistence crops with the strength of communal labor, many farmers seek cash for their crops and grow them with the help of hired labor. Farmers who are not successful leave the villages and go to work in the city. The work of traditional farmers and women is seen as inferior in a society that now has MTV and other fruits of capitalism. Many goods, such as food, clothing, and building materials, are now imported; this not only makes traditional goods less valuable but also introduces people to potentially hazardous products about which they have little information. The movement of young people to cities and the exposure of villagers to new lifestyles mean that fewer Ladakhi are following traditional marriage customs or entering monasticism. The result has been a significant rise in population. Because Ladakh cannot support a large population without outside help, this will translate into a need for even more imported goods.

Even in agriculture, the Ladakhi have seen many changes, some of them implemented by government development policies. For example, waterwheels were traditionally used to grind grain. Now, diesel-powered mills have been introduced. The new mills grind grain much faster, but they are less convenient; villagers must bring their grain from the village to the central mill to be ground and then must pay for the service. Also, the increased speed of the diesel mill heats the grain and reduces its nutritional value. The mill also causes pollution as it spits fumes into the air.

The Jersey cow is replacing the yak and dzo as the main domestic animal. Although the cows produce ten times as much milk as yaks, they are not as well adapted to the Ladakhi environment. They are not accustomed to such high altitudes or to walking up the steep mountain trails, so they are more time-consuming and costly to maintain, needing special shelter and fodder.

In what could be a disastrous move, the Indian army has planted trees and other vegetation throughout Ladakh in an attempt to add oxygen to the air and make life easier for the soldiers and other outsiders who have come to live there. Many Ladakhi say that the trees and plants have caused more rainfall than is normal; if true, this could disrupt the traditional way of life even more by changing farming practices and even architectural designs that had been especially suited to the dry climate.

Looking to the Future

Ladakh has long enjoyed its reputation as an undisturbed mountain paradise. In fact, it has sometimes been called "the last

Because of its peaceful, remote location, Ladakh has been lauded as "heaven on earth." The very traits that made it so popular are disappearing as more and more tourists flock to what they consider to be paradise.

Shangri-la," an imaginary land created by James Hilton in his novel *Lost Horizon*. It is understood to mean a remote paradise or utopia on earth.

With its otherwordly emptiness, its healthy and peaceful people, and its spiritual aura, Ladakh as it existed for hundreds of years may indeed have been many people's idea of Shangri-la. But today, with its increasing roster of modern problems and growing pains, Ladakh is starting to look more like the rest of the world. The question is not whether Ladakh should be opened up to the modern world. That will happen no matter what.

Exposure to the outside world is already taking place; the question is whether that exposure will highlight and enrich traditional Ladakhi institutions, or whether it will destroy them. Similarly, the question is not whether or not economic development will take place, but whether the path to development can be navigated by people who value the special needs and perspectives of the Ladakhi people and seek to preserve their rich and complex heritage. Nongovernmental organizations in India are already working to lay out a plan for Ladakh that works with, not against, traditional ways. The Indian government would do well to work with Ladakhi and experts on Ladakh to develop a plan in which the Ladakhi people can truly be the beneficiaries of development.

One of the problems facing those who are struggling to save traditional Ladakh is that many young people—the most crucial resource in any society—have been caught up in the growth of cities and capitalism and now look upon village farm life as backward and distasteful. They, too, must be convinced of the inherent value of traditional ways of life and work to preserve them even if they themselves do not want to return to the farms. In an encouraging trend, some of these young people have pursued modern education and have chosen to apply that education to helping their own people.

The Dalai Lama, the spiritual leader of Tibetan Buddhists, has written that he is optimistic about the ability of the Ladakhi to overcome the challenges they face. He has described how Tibetan monasteries have strengthened their connections to

Ladakhi monasteries in an attempt to bolster the monastic system and the traditional education provided by monks. As the Dalai Lama points out, the Ladakhi people cannot be denied the fruits of modernization. They should, however, have a say about how modernization and development take their course in their own land.

Helena Norberg-Hodge, a Swede who is fluent in the Ladakhi language and has lived among the Ladakhi for years, has taken a great interest in how development has negatively affected the people. She encourages instead the concept of counterdevelopment, in which the negative effects of development are dealt with and a more ecologically sound model is explored. She has worked with the Ladakhi to explore alternative programs of development, such as the use of solar power and hydraulic pumps, and to educate them about environmental issues. She was alarmed that the Ladakhi received so little information about the potential hazards of products like infant formula or pesticides. By 1980, Norberg-Hodge's work had evolved into the Ladakh Project, which in 1991 became the International Society for Ecology and Culture. The goals of the project are to promote ecological and community-based development and to encourage political and economic decision-making at the local level. Along with a group of concerned Ladakhi, Norberg-Hodge helped to found the Ladakh Ecological Development Group in 1983. The group promotes new solutions and makes its work known to policymakers in India and abroad. The Students' Educational and Cultural Movement of Ladakh is another group working to ease Ladakh's journey on the path of modernization.

Can a few decades of modern pressures destroy something as precious as the way of life of a people? The work of Norberg-Hodge and of the Ladakhi themselves points to the fact that a downward spiral need not be Ladakh's destiny. Traditional Ladakhi values of adaptability, cooperation, compassion, and understanding of the environment will be put to the test more than ever as the people face a grave challenge to their lifestyle.▲

NEIGHBORING PEOPLES

THE HIMALAYA MOUNTAIN RANGE SEPARATES THE LADAKHI from the people of Kashmir, who number about 8 million. The Kashmiri language is a member of the Dardic family of languages but has also borrowed heavily from Sanskrit and Hindi-Urdu, both Indo-European languages. Few written works exist in Kashmiri because of difficulties in transcribing the language into written form.

The **Kashmiri** have endured a great deal of religious and political strife in the last 50 years, largely because of the partition of India, which was administered by the British in 1947. The ruling family of Kashmir at the time was Hindu and wanted to be a part of predominantly Hindu India; yet the majority of Kashmir's population was Muslim. When Kashmir was made part of India rather than the Muslim nation of Pakistan, many Kashmiri Muslims were enraged. Three wars followed the partition, and conflict still rages. Some nationalists want Kashmir to be declared an independent state.

To the east of Ladakh lies Tibet, home of four million **Tibetans**. Tibet fell under the control of the Chinese government in 1959 and is now known as the Tibet Autonomous Region (TAR). Chinese repression and settlement of Chinese people in Tibet have displaced thousands of Tibetans, some of whom have settled in Ladakh. The Chinese occupation of Tibet has provoked worldwide condemnation. The Dalai Lama, the Tibetan Buddhists' spiritual leader and Tibet's secular leader, fled to India with 80,000 followers when Chinese troops arrived in Tibet in 1959. He has been a powerful spokesman for the rights of the Tibetan people.

Most Tibetans are sedentary farmers, like the Ladakhi. They keep yaks, sheep, goats, and horses, and their diet is almost the same as that of the Ladakhi. Polyandry and polygyny are occasionally practiced in traditional Tibetan society, and women enjoy a large degree of independence and freedom. The Tibetan language is in the Sino-Tibetan language family.

Tibet also has a nomadic population. They call themselves **Drobka** and inhabit the western and northwestern Chang Tang plateau, bordering on Ladakh. Like the Ladakhi, the Drobka have developed a pattern of subsistence that has enabled them to survive for centuries in an environment that seems to offer nothing. The Chang Tang is considered dangerous by many Tibetans in villages and cities; yet the nomads travel long distances across it, sometimes alone. The nomads' most valuable animal is the sheep, which provides them with wool, meat, and fleece for winter robes.

Nomadic Tibetans hold an annual festival in honor of their spiritual leader, the Dalai Lama.

Nomadic pastoralism is practiced in few places in the world. Tibetan nomads are one of a handful of peoples who maintain this way of life. It is not an easy life. A snowstorm can wipe out a family's herd; the nomads must milk and herd their animals no matter what the weather, and with a winter that can be eight months long, the weather is often bitterly cold. Home-base sites consist of clumps of yak-hair tents, one family to each tent.

Chinese occupation of Tibet took its toll on traditional nomad culture. As part of the Cultural Revolution in the late

The Chinese occupation of Tibet forced thousands of Tibetans to flee to neighboring countries. These Tibetan children live in a refugee camp in Ladakh.

1960s, the Communist Chinese government forced the nomads to form communes and discouraged the practice of Buddhism. Nomads were required to turn over all livestock and tools to the commune, and the commune dictated the work they would do. This system was completely foreign to the nomads' traditional way of life. The Chinese leaders also tried to destroy aspects of traditional Tibetan culture. The much-hated communes were eliminated in 1976 with the end of the Cultural Revolution, but the nomads still fear government involvement in their lives. The Chinese have pressured many nomads to abandon their pastoral lands and adopt a more sedentary lifestyle in Ladakh.▲

FACTS ABOUT THE LADAKHI

Population: 150,000

Location: Northern India

Environment: High-altitude desert, with major mountains

Climate: Long winters, short summers

Rainfall: 3 inches per year

Language: Bodhi

Religion: Buddhism and Islam

Main Activities: Agriculture, trading

Main Crops: Barley, peas, turnips, potatoes

Domestic Animals: Sheep, goats, donkeys, horses, dzo

Game Animals: Blue sheep, wolf, snow leopard, wild goat, red
bear, wild horse, lynx, antelope, gazelle, marmot, ibex, hare

GLOSSARY

cavalry Troops mounted on horseback.

chang Home-brewed barley beer.

frugality The quality of practicing economy in the use of resources.

hemoglobin A necessary substance in the red blood cells.

hypoxia Deficiency of oxygen in the tissues of the body.

lama Tibetan (Mahayana) Buddhist monk.

partition Political division of a country into two separate nations.

monastery Establishment for monks.

phasphun Group of families pledged to help one another in time of need.

phu Grazing land.

plateau Level land surface raised above the adjacent land.

polyandry Practice of having more than one husband.

polygyny Practice of having more than one wife.

shaman Person who communicates with the spirit world.

thresh To separate grain from straw.

FOR FURTHER READING

Ahluwalia, H.P.S. *Hermit Kingdom Ladakh*. Honesdale, PA: Himalayan Books, 1987.

Apte, Robert Z. *Three Kingdoms on the Roof of the World*. Berkeley, CA: Parallax Press, 1990.

Beall, Cynthia M., and Goldstein, Melvyn. *Nomads of Western Tibet: The Survival of a Way of Life*. Hong Kong: Odyssey Productions, 1990.

Crook, John, and Ostmaston, Henry, eds. *Himalayan Buddhist Villages: Environment, Resources, Society and Religious Life in Zansgkar, Ladakh*. Bristol: University of Bristol, 1994.

Gonen, Amiram, ed. *The Encyclopedia of the Peoples of the World*. New York: Henry Holt, 1993.

Jaitly, Jaya, ed. *Crafts of Kashmir, Jammu, and Ladakh*. New York: Abbeville Press, 1990.

Kapur, Tegbahadur. *Ladakh, the Wonderland: A Geographical, Historical, and Sociological Study*. New Delhi: Mittal Publications, 1987.

Norberg-Hodge, Helena. *Ancient Futures: Learning from Ladakh*. San Francisco: Sierra Club, 1991.

INDEX

63

Photo Credits: ©Anako Editions/H. Lam Duc
Layout and Design: Kim Sonsky